The
Battle of Hastings

Jane Shuter

www.heinemann.co.uk/library
Visit our website to find out more information about **Heinemann Library** books.

To order:
☎ Phone 44 (0) 1865 888066
🖹 Send a fax to 44 (0) 1865 314091
💻 Visit the Heinemann Bookshop at www.heinemann.co.uk/library to browse our catalogue and order online.

First published in Great Britain by Heinemann Library, Halley Court, Jordan Hill, Oxford OX2 8EJ, part of Harcourt Education.
Heinemann is a registered trademark of Harcourt Education Ltd.

Editorial: Lucy Thunder and Helen Cox
Design: David Poole and Geoff Ward
Illustrations: Ron Tiner
Picture Research: Hannah Taylor
Production: Séverine Ribierre

Originated by Repro Multi Warna
Printed and bound in Hong Kong, China by South China Printing

ISBN 0 431 12344 6
07 06 05 04 03
10 9 8 7 6 5 4 3 2 1

British Library Cataloguing in Publication Data
Shuter, Jane
How do we know about the Battle of Hastings?
942'.021
A full catalogue record for this book is available from the British Library.

Acknowledgements
Art Archive/Musée de la Tapisserie Bayeux/Dagli Orti p5; Art Archive p26; British Museum p22; Corbis pp24 (Adam Woolfitt), 25 (Charles Lenar Michael Holford pp4, 18, 19; J Sampton/Wells Cathedral p23; Topham/Museum of London pp20, 21; Tudor Photography p27.

Cover photograph of the Bayeux Tapestry, reproduced with permission of Corbis (Nik Wheeler).

The publishers would like to thank Rebecca Vick for her assistance in the preparation of this book

Every effort has been made to contact copyright holders of any material reproduced in this book. Any omissions will be rectified in subsequent printings if notice is given to the publishers.

Contents

Any words shown in the text in bold, **like this**, are explained in the Glossary.

Two promises

On 5 January 1066, the King of England, Edward the **Confessor**, died. He had already told William, Duke of Normandy, in France, that he could be the next King of England.

As he was dying, Edward also told an English **earl**, Harold Godwinson, that he could be king. Edward had promised two people they could **rule** England!

Who will be king?

The English **earls** always chose the King of England. Most of them wanted the king to be English. They crowned Harold as king on 6 January 1066.

William of Normandy was angry. He wanted to **rule** England. He decided to **invade**. He got soldiers, horses, weapons and boats ready to sail to England.

Another problem

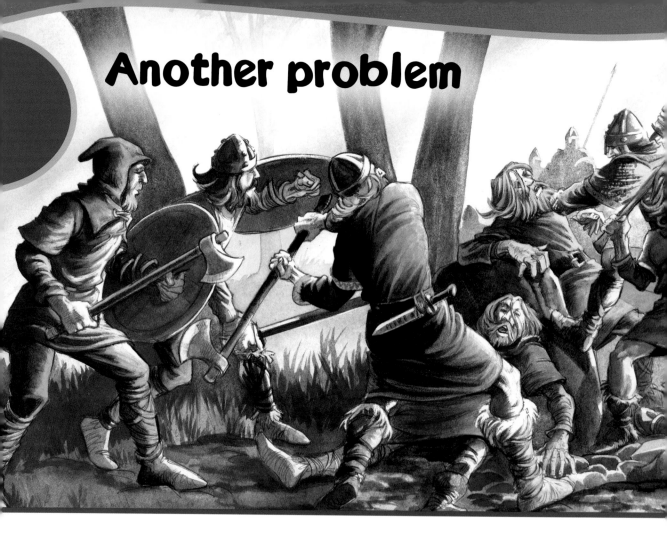

William was not the only **ruler** who wanted to **invade** England and be king. Harald Hadrada, King of Norway, was planning just the same thing.

Hadrada's army landed on the coast of
England, near York, in September 1066.
King Harold marched north to meet
him. He beat Hadrada's army in a battle
at Stamford Bridge.

Invasion!

While King Harold was still in the north of England, William and his army sailed from France. They landed on the south coast of England, near Hastings.

King Harold marched south quickly. In London more soldiers joined him, but they did not stop to rest. When they reached William's army, near Hastings, they were tired.

The Battle of Hastings

The Battle of Hastings began on 14 October 1066. Both armies had about 7000 soldiers. William's Norman army had **archers** and **horsemen** as well as ordinary soldiers.

Harold's army was on top of a hill, so William's soldiers had to struggle uphill to fight them. When the Normans ran away, Harold's men followed them.

William wins

William's soldiers tricked Harold's men. Once they were at the bottom of the hill, the Normans turned around and started fighting. Harold was killed.

By the end of the day, William's army had won. William marched to London. His soldiers burned towns and stole food and belongings as they went.

William the ruler

The **earls** heard what William's army had done and agreed William could be king. He was crowned on 25 December 1066 as William I, 'the **Conqueror**'.

William **ruled** England until he died in 1087. He made English people use the French language. The Normans also built castles to keep their land well **protected**.

How do we know?

RVNT QVIERANT CVM

This is part of the Bayeux **Tapestry**. It shows what happened from before Edward the **Confessor's** death up to William I's **coronation**.

The Bayeaux Tapestry was made for the
Normans after the Battle of Hastings. It
only tells their side of the story. It was
hung in Bayeux Cathedral, Normandy,
in 1077.

Armour and weapons

Some **armour** and weapons have survived from the Battle of Hastings. The armour **protected** the soldiers, but was very heavy. The picture shows an **Anglo-Saxon** helmet.

20

Both sides in the Battle of Hastings fought with swords, axes and long spears. The Norman **archers** also fired arrows at Harold's army.

Coins and statues

Every new **ruler** of England had their picture stamped onto coins. This coin shows William the **Conqueror** soon after he was crowned king.

This is part of a statue of William. It is on the outside of Wells Cathedral, in south-west England. There are many statues of William in England.

Norman buildings

William was a Norman, so English people did not like him. The **earls** only helped him **rule** when he gave them castles and power. The Tower of London, shown here, was built by the Normans.

In 1070, William had this grand stone church built to celebrate his victory at the Battle of Hastings. It took 24 years to finish. It is now called Battle Abbey.

Writings

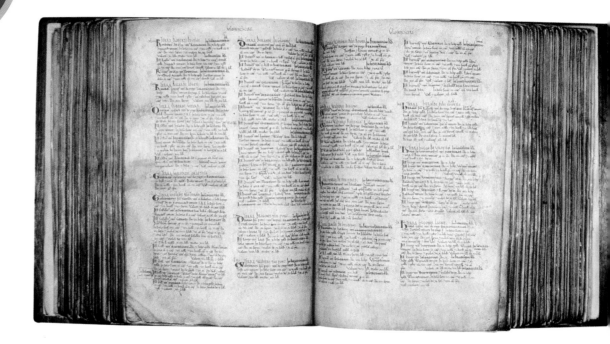

William wanted to **tax** his people fairly. His men made lists of what people owned and put them into the Domesday Book. It was used to work out everyone's taxes.

The Battle of Hastings changed England so much that people still write about it. It changed how the country was run and even what language people spoke.

Timeline

1064 Harold Godwinson visits William in Normandy. Later, William says that Harold promised to support him as the next King of England at this meeting.

5 January 1066 Edward the **Confessor** dies.

6 January 1066 Harold Godwinson made King of England by the English **earls**.

April 1066 King Harold hears that Harald Hadrada, King of Norway, plans to **invade**.

September 1066 King Harold of England moves north and gathers an army. Harald Hadrada's army invades.

25 September 1066 King Harold wins the Battle of Stamford Bridge against Hadrada's army.

28 September 1066 William, Duke of Normandy, invades England.

14 October 1066 Battle of Hastings. King Harold dies.

25 December 1066 William of Normandy is crowned King William I of England.

9 September 1087 William I dies.

Biographies

Harold Godwinson (Harold II)

Harold Godwinson was born in about 1022. He was Edward the **Confessor's** brother-in-law. He was a good soldier and war leader. The English earls made him King of England in January 1066. He was killed at the Battle of Hastings in October 1066.

Harald Hadrada

Harald Hadrada was born in about 1016. In about 1030 he and his family were driven out of Norway. Hadrada became a **mercenary**, moving from country to country with his men. He became King of Norway in 1047. He died at the Battle of Stamford Bridge in September 1066.

William, Duke of Normandy (William I)

William of Normandy was born in about 1028. He became Duke of Normandy in 1035 when he was only seven years old. He was Edward the Confessor's great-nephew. He invaded England in 1066, won the Battle of Hastings and was crowned King of England. William **ruled** for 21 years. He died in 1087.

Glossary

Anglo-Saxon people living in England before the Normans invaded

archer soldier who fires arrows from a bow

armour clothes that protect a soldier's body during fighting. Armour was often made from metal, leather or padded cloth.

confessor person who owns up to doing wrong, usually by talking to God or to a priest

conqueror someone who wins against enemies in battle

coronation ceremony where a person is given a crown to show they are the ruler of a country

earl rich and powerful English man

horsemen in an army, soldiers riding on horses to fight

invade to send an army into another country to take it over and rule it

mercenary well-trained soldier who fights for whoever will pay him

protect keep safe from harm

rule to lead or be in charge of a country. A king or queen is a ruler.

tapestry piece of cloth with a picture or pattern stitched onto it. The Bayeaux Tapestry is made from linen cloth, stitched with coloured wools. It was begun after the Battle of Hastings and took about eleven years to make.

tax money that people in a country have to pay to whoever is running that country

Further reading

You may need help to read these books:

Great Events: The Battle of Hastings, Franklin Watts, 2001

1066 – A Decisive Battle, Richard Tames, Heinemann Library, 1998

Index

Titles in the *How Do we Know About ...?* series include:

Hardback 0 431 12344 6

Hardback 0 431 12346 2

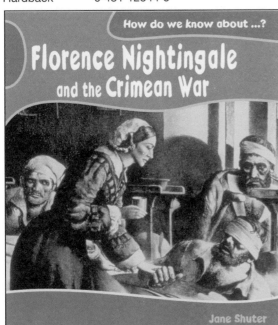

Hardback 0 431 12345 4

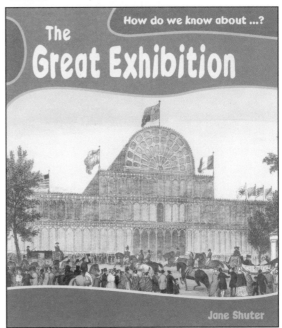

Hardback 0 431 12347 0

Find out about the other titles in this series on our website www.heinemann.co.uk/library